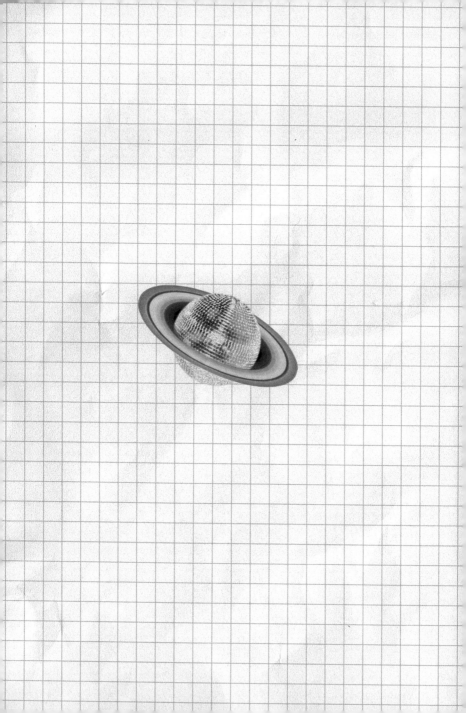

Here to Shine: Born for a Reason
Published by Parent Cue, a division of The reThink Group, Inc.
5870 Charlotte Lane, Suite 300
Cumming, GA 30040 U.S.A.

All Scripture quotations, unless otherwise noted, are taken from the Holy Bible, New International Reader's Version®, NIrV® Copyright © 1995, 1996, 1998, 2014 by Biblica, used by permission of Zondervan. All rights reserved worldwide. www.Zondervan.com The "NIrV" and "New International Reader's Version" are trademarks registered in the United States Patent and Trademark Office by Biblica, Inc.

Scripture quotations marked "NIV" are taken from the Holy Bible, New International Version®, NIV®. Copyright © 1973, 1978, 1984, 2011 by Biblica, Inc. permission of Zondervan. All rights reserved worldwide. www.Zondervan.com The "NIV" and "New International Version" are trademarks registered in the United States Patent and Trademark Office by Biblica, Inc.

Scripture quotations marked "ERV" are taken from the HOLY BIBLE: EASY-TO-READ VERSION © 2001 by World Bible Translation Center, Inc. and used by permission.

Interested in buying devotionals for the kids in your church or community? Get discounted rates on quantities of 10 or more at parentcuestore.org or orangestore.org.

ISBN: 978-1-63570-211-8

©2024 The reThink Group, Inc.

Content & Framework Direction: Reggie Joiner
Creative Direction: Leslie Mack
Experience Direction: Hannah Joiner
Art Direction & Collage: Ashley Shugart
Writing & Editing Team: Leslie Mack, Reggie Joiner, Hannah Joiner,
Ashley Litton, Lauren Sellers, Karen Wilson & Mike Tiemann
Design & Layout Team: Ashley Shugart, Brannon Powell & Elizabeth Hildreth
Management Team: Brian Sharp & Mike Jeffries

Printed in China
First Edition 2024

1 2 3 4 5 6 7 8 9 10

03/01/24

A 28-Day Devotional for Kids

Let's Party!

HERE TO SHINE

BORN FOR A REASON

LESLIE MACK & FRIENDS

PS PARENT CUE

START HERE

What's up, friend? Welcome to a new book!

Well, this is actually not just "a book." This is YOUR book. Written just for you.

That's why there's that HUGE space over there to write, design, decorate, scribble, collage, or even secret-code YOUR name and leave your mark!

Now, you could just read this book . . . but that would be boring. It would be even better if you EXPERIENCED this book.

Turn the page to see five ways to unlock this book.

You are remarkable. Yes, you are extraordinary! God made you and everyone else that way. Don't believe it? Just keep reading.

Signed,

Leslie and a bunch of my friends

This book belongs to:

Audree Lancaster

LET'S PARTY

5

5 Ways to Unlock This Book

look for stickers

When you see:

you can discover a big idea to help you shine even brighter! Follow the stickers throughout this book and look for how these ideas connect.

tell your parent

Tell your adult human person all about this book. Show them a few pages and rip this square out and give it to them:

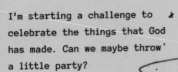

I'm starting a challenge to celebrate the things that God has made. Can we maybe throw a little party?

be a party starter

We saved the best for last: every "Day 7" in this book is all about celebrating something God has done, so throw a mini-party! Get ready to be a party starter!

6

create your time capsule

Anytime you see:

grab some supplies and your time capsule! Your time capsule can be a shoebox, a lunch box, an old cereal box, one of those weird tins with cookies on the front that never actually has cookies inside, or one you make. Whatever you use, we're going to fill it with amazing things we can use to start a party.

count to 28

If you can count to 28, you can make it to the end of this book! Whether you do one page a day, one page a week, or one page a month, these 28 days will help you see the wonder of God's story and how you fit into it. Keep track here:

HABIT TRACKER

Week 1

◯ ◯ ◯ ◯ ◯ ◯ ◯

Week 2

◯ ◯ ◯ ◯ ◯ ◯ ◯

Week 3

◯ ◯ ◯ ◯ ◯ ◯ ◯

Week 4

◯ ◯ ◯ ◯ ◯ ◯ ◯

WHEN THE STA

RS
WERE BORN

DAY 4	DAY 5	DAY 6	DAY 7
Explore the galaxies	God is here	You are known	God stopped to party

9

The STARS were born to blaze the night
Majestically designed
God spoke the words, "Let there be light"
The world began to shine

Stars glimmered and beamed and burned so bright
in galaxies above
and heaven's mirrors showed the world
the wonder of God's love

The stars were born to POINT the way
and navigate what God has made
Here to shine, here to say
God is good, God is great

Countless lights illuminate
God knows them each by name
Creation started, then it stopped
so God could pause to celebrate
The things that God had done
'cause God is good and God is great

At the beginning of the world, God created light.

A long time ago, beyond the galaxies, far, far away, before there was anything, there was God.

And God was up to something...
Creating. Planning. Designing. Building.

But what was God creating? For who?
And what could God's first act of creation back then possibly say to you today?

Let's find out together.

God made a lot of amazing things

stars are born for a reason

Do you know what it takes for someone to become a star ...
basketball player?
gymnast?
dancer?
LEGO® builder?

If you made a list of what it takes to shine like a star,
it would probably include a lot of things like ...
extra practice, working out, good coaches, better equipment,
natural instincts, physical coordination, a healthy diet,
and Nikes®.

**But what if the same thing that makes someone a star
is actually the same thing that makes a *star* a star?**

It probably sounds kind of out there, but we *are* talking about the
cosmos.

And maybe you haven't noticed lately, but you and the stars have a
lot in common. Humans and stars are both made from a mixture of
the same gases and elements.

And there is one very critical thing they both need.

MADE

So back to the question,
what makes a *star* a star?

Here's a hint:
It's the reason a star is born.
It's the reason a star is round.
It's the reason a star exists for thousands or millions
or trillions of years.
It's even the reason you can breathe air.
And it's an invisible force.

Just to be clear, this "invisible force" we are talking about is not
God. Sure, God made the world, and God made the stars. But God
is bigger than this invisible force we're talking about because God
made it too.

And here's something else to think about:
What if God made the stars to shine a light so you could
understand things about God?

What if God made you to be curious and ask questions about
things like the stars?

So, have you figured it out?
Do you know what makes a *star* a star?

Gravity

DAY 1

light shows you...

Yep, it's gravity. Sure, gravity isn't the only thing that makes a star a star, but it's an important one. The most simple definition of a star is "a sphere of gas held together by its own gravity."

Without gravity, stars would never be born, the world would not orbit the sun, and you couldn't play basketball. Just Google it. Watch a YouTube video. Do some reading about it.

When God said, "Let there be light" and created the sun, moon, and stars to shine, God did something else to keep everything in place. God created gravity.

The same God Who said it was good to create the stars evidently thinks it's good for you to ask questions about the stars. Here is something God wanted written down in an ancient book—the Bible—so you would know that we can learn secrets from the stars:

> The heavens declare the glory of God;
>   the skies proclaim the work of his hands ...
>   night after night they reveal knowledge
>   (Psalm 19:1-2, NIV).

What do you think that means? There's apparently something about the galaxies that helps us understand more about God and life. Even the stars in the night sky can actually "reveal knowledge." (That just means they can help us discover things.)

14

It's true. We know a lot more now about life because people asked questions about the stars for thousands of years.

Studying the stars has helped us understand more about navigating, measuring time, flying airplanes, weather patterns, pollution, farming, electronics, and hundreds of other things.

So, keep asking questions about how stars are born.

Maybe God put the stars here to shine to help you know how to shine.

gravity helps me

Think about the things that gravity helps you do and write them inside of the balloons!

DAY 2 keep looking...

wow, look at the stars

You made it to Day 2!

Want to know something? You have a superpower you might not be aware of.

You are a time-traveler. No, really! You can see into the past.

Like really, REALLY far into the past. Like before last week, before your fourth birthday, before your grandmother was born, and before dinosaurs.

Every night, you get the chance to travel back in time to see the past ... way, far back in time. (Yeah, unfortunately too far back to record that trick shot you landed once.)

How can you time-travel? Simple.

Tonight when the sun sets, put on your shoes (they don't have to be Marty McFlys*). Go outside and stare into the sky until you see a star.

 Time travel! Amazing, right!?

*Go ask your parent or grandparent what Marty McFlys are

Okay, maybe not that impressive on the surface, but ...

This may blow your mind: Stars are soooo far away, it could take billions of light-years for the light from that star to get to your eyeball today.

Which means ... the stars you see tonight are really stars from the past—maybe billions of light-years from the past.

How is that even possible?! God only knows.

In the galaxy, time and space and the things we see all work together to tell us something today. Here's some more from the ancient text we have already read in Psalm 19:1-4 (NIV):

> The heavens declare the glory of God;
>> the skies proclaim the work of his hands.
> Day after day they pour forth speech;
>> night after night they reveal knowledge.
> They have no speech, they use no words;
>> no sound is heard from them.
> Yet their voice goes out into all the earth,
>> their words to the ends of the world.
> In the heavens God has pitched a tent for the sun.

The sky talks without talking.
The stars are trying to tell us something.

The more we look, the more we discover.

17

DAY 2

seeing what God did...

So, do a little time-traveling tonight.

It's wild to think that maybe, from the very beginning, God designed the stars so far away in the past just for a chance to tell you every night—in the present—that He's been thinking about you. That's right, God's been thinking about you since forever and into the future.

It's amazing that something so old
(that a message so old) could be . . .
so bright.
so powerful.
so good.
so mysterious and wondrous that you never have to
stop being amazed by it.
so vast that it never runs out and always has something to say.
so constant that you can count on it every night so far
and every night that's left.

And that's just the stars you CAN see.

If the stars you CAN see carry the message of a timeless love,
imagine what the God Who made the galaxies you CAN'T see is
trying to say to say to you!

I've already loved you forever.

18

WHEN THE STARS WERE BORN

WOW!

Every time you look at the stars, you are seeing back in time.

And now, every time you look at the stars, you will be reminded that God has loved you forever.

And that's something that only a really big, creative God Who existed before time could do.

If God could be trusted before time began to design the sky to show up every night with a message for you, maybe God is big enough to be trusted tonight and every night.

DAY 2

if we keep looking...

If you wonder if God can be trusted, put on your shoes and go visit with the stars.

God used stars to lock away this wonder, beauty, and mystery before time began to send a message to you each night:

- ▶ I am here.
- ▶ I think the world of you.
- ▶ I created a world just for you.
- ▶ I would have (I have) moved heaven and earth to tell you that you mean the world to me.
- ▶ I will sculpt galaxies to write a love note to you.
- ▶ I will paint night skies to remind you that I think the world of you.
- ▶ I will draw stars to whisper over and over, "You are special to me."

constellations

When you take a look at the stars, do you see any patterns that make a shape? A group of stars that looks like a shape and has been given a name is called a constellation.

To the right is a cluster of stars. Do you see any shapes? Go ahead, connect some stars and draw your own constellation!

...we will discover more

what's something you wonder about?

imagine what God can do

Be on the lookout for this:

If you think about it, stars are kind of like God's time capsule.

A time capsule is an indestructible container that people fill with important objects and a special message. They lock it away, trusting that one day when it's opened, they'll be able to communicate with people in the future!

Why are we talking about time capsules?

Well . . .

TIME CAPSULE

God used stars to lock away incredible wonders and mysteries about the universe that have existed before the world began. Then God positioned the stars to send a message to you each night. It's as if God is saying . . .

> "I created the stars to shine so you can see what I did long before you were born."

> "Every star is an invitation to imagine things you haven't seen yet."

"The reason you can imagine what you haven't seen yet is because I created you in My image. So, I don't want you to only imagine what I have done or what I can do. I want you to imagine what YOU can do."

Isn't it crazy? Since the beginning of the universe, God designed stars to keep shining from the past so you can see their light in your present, everyday world. If what you see now happened potentially billions of years before you were born, then that means God has been thinking about you for forever. God cared about your future when you didn't even exist.

That's why stars are like God's time capsule.

They were here to send you a message when you showed up.

And the reason stars are so . . .

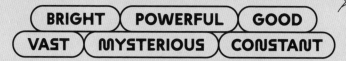

BRIGHT | POWERFUL | GOOD
VAST | MYSTERIOUS | CONSTANT

. . . is because God didn't want you to miss seeing what He can do. God also didn't want you to miss seeing something about you.

If God created a star to shine like that, then God definitely created you to do some amazing things.

DAY 3

you are bright!

You were put here to shine just like the stars.

The same God who said, "Let there be light" in the beginning of the world also said, "Let us make mankind in our image" (Genesis 1:26, NIV).

Then when God finished creating the moon, sun, stars, oceans, mountains, animals, and people, God saw that what He had created was very good.

Something good happened when the world was born.

And something good happened when you were born too.

time-travel to vacation

If you took a vacation and time-traveled thousands of years into the past, what would you bring? (You can choose things from your life today.)

Write your answers in the shapes to the right!

WHAT
IF?

Pets:

One sport or game:

Favorite
outfit:

Three friends:

Two snacks:

n't worry, your family
also going with you
this imaginary time-
aveling vacation.

One song:

God cares about you finding your way

explore the galaxies

Before there was a map app on phones . . .
Before there were physical maps . . .
Before there were roads, and highways, and paths . . .
how did people get from way over here to way, waaaaay over there
without getting lost?

Explorers and travelers of all kinds didn't have maps on phones;
they had stars.
And they depended on them.

Stars helped predict the weather.
Stars provided light.
Stars made food grow.
(Well, one star in particular—that big one we call the sun.)
And stars helped humans travel far distances.

So, instead of looking down at a phone screen,
they looked up at the night sky.

Instead of a GPS satellite 12,550 miles above our heads, they used
stars dozens of miles away.

It's like God was saying,
"Here. These are for you.
To make sure you can always find your way."

WHEN THE STARS WERE BORN

The cool thing about stars is that stars don't just shine; they point.

They point to history and time. For astrophysicists and astronauts, stars point the way for shuttles and rockets. For people escaping harm, stars have pointed the way to freedom and safety. For wise men, stars pointed the way to a Savior (but more about that later).

The stars may look like chaos—random, sparkly, distant chaos. But when you explore the galaxies, you find a highly organized system of math, science, measurements, degrees, percentages, gases, liquids, temperatures, colors, and reactions.

These are all held in place to create a guide that has helped people find their way and go where no one has gone before—for thousands of years.

Stars remind us:

- ❱ Sometimes, you have to find your way in the dark, but you're not alone.
- ❱ Sometimes, you have to connect the dots and tell a story to help you remember the way.
- ❱ Sometimes, you have to use what you have to inspire you to keep going.

The stars remind you that God knows where you are and wants to help you get to where you're going.

DAY 4

`follow the light...`

As long as you can wait for the night and see the stars, you can take it as a promise that God cares about you so much that He doesn't want you to feel lost.

star maze

Follow the dashed lines through the stars and match the items that go together.

LOVE

DAY 5

God is here

Did you know that God designed light so it is always around you even when you can't see it? Even when it's really dark? How do we know? Because some animals and insects were created with night vision. They have a tiny mirror in their eyes that helps them see at night. It's a layer of tissue called a tapetum, and it has cells that contain tiny crystals to reflect light that's invisible to human eyes.

Have you ever seen a dog, cat, or deer's eyes at night when a light is shining on them? Their eyes seem to glow, don't they? Their tapetum is shining. That's how they are able to see in the dark. Even when we can't see the light, there are still enough light particles floating in the air for some animals to see.

So, God not only created light so you can see where to go. God also created light so you would know that when you can't see the light, the light is still there. Whenever you look out at the night, remember there's always light shining, even if you can't see it with your own eyes.

Some stars are so far away that you need a telescope to see them. Some light waves are invisible unless you wear night-vision goggles. But there is always light all around you wherever you go.
God is always with you wherever you go too.
Since the beginning of the world, God has promised to be here with you.

WHEN THE STARS WERE BORN

HERE

If you get scared, start to worry, are hurt, or feel alone ... you can trust that God is with you, even if you can't see God.

Here's something God promised a leader named Joshua thousands of years ago:

> "Be strong and brave. Do not be afraid. Do not lose hope. I am the LORD your God. I will be with you everywhere you go" (Joshua 1:9, NIrV).

You may not have a tapetum to see in the dark like a deer, but you can be as sure as the stars are still shining that God is with you, whatever happens.

talk and listen

Even though you can't see in the dark, you know what you CAN do?! You can talk and you can listen!

What is a song that helps you remember that God is here with you?

....

....

Check out these songs that might help too!

Who is someone you can talk to who helps you remember that God is here?

....

....

The next time you're feeling scared, worried, hurt, or alone, try listening to a song or talking to someone you trust who can remind you that the light is still shining. God is still here.

DAY 6 God knows every star...

you are known

Have you ever tried to count the stars?

Scientists have been trying to figure out
how many stars are in the night sky for a long time.

Almost 2,000 years ago, a Greek astronomer named Ptolemy
charted 1,022 stars. Almost 1,500 years later, another astronomer
named Johann Bayer decided that Ptolemy had counted wrong.

According to Bayer, there were more than 1,022 stars.
He claimed in 1603 that he had actually found and named
2,000 stars.

Then, six years later, something happened that changed
everything about how scientists count the stars: the telescope was
invented.

When a man named Galileo looked at the night sky
through a telescope, he made an amazing discovery:

There were more stars behind the stars they couldn't
see with their eyes.

And every time scientists would improve the telescope,
do you know what they saw?

32

Even more stars beyond those stars.

Finally, in 1990, scientists designed the Hubble telescope to travel on a rocket ship and take pictures in space.

Can you guess what they discovered?

There are more stars than we can imagine.
Maybe more stars than we can actually count.

Scientists estimate there could be as many as 200,000,000,000,000,000,000,000 stars.

That's a lot more than 1,022 stars.

Read this out loud so you can hear what that number sounds like:
Two hundred billion trillion.

You know how many stars that is?
It is 10 times more than the number
of cups of water in all the oceans on earth.

Thousands of years ago, humans could only gaze at
the night sky and wonder, "How many stars are there?"

And one human, inspired by the Creator of the universe,

W

HERE TO SHINE

WEEK ONE

HERE TO SHINE

WEEK ONE

HERE TO SHINE

WEEK ONE

SHINE

DAY 6 — God sees the stars. God sees you...

looking only at the stars he could see, wrote these words about God:

> He counts the stars
>   and knows each of them by name (Psalm 147:4, ERV).

When this was written, humans had no idea how many stars there actually are. And now we only have a best guess. So, if God knows the name of nearly 200 billion trillion stars, then don't you think God knows you too?

The next time you look up at the night sky, start counting. Imagine the stars you CAN'T see.

Then, remember that the God Who made the stars sees and cares about you.

stars by name

Here are just a few of the stars that humans have named! See if you can find their names in the word search.

WHEN THE
STARS
WERE BO
LOVE

CAPELLA	BETELGEUSE	NEMBUS	SIRIUS
TEJAT	DENEB	ALCOR	POLARIS
OKAB	PROCYON	SPICA	SAIPH
MINTAKA	ANTARES	MEISSA	SEGIN
VEGA	ALDEBARAN	REGULUS	

```
W  B  A  N  R  D  P  R  O  C  Y  O  N  M
U  B  N  E  E  X  X  A  L  C  O  R  R  Y
S  C  T  M  G  D  F  Y  F  S  E  G  I  N
A  A  A  B  U  E  T  E  J  A  T  O  P  I
B  P  R  U  L  N  X  E  A  V  O  R  R  H
E  E  E  S  U  E  S  N  M  Q  F  K  G  G
T  L  S  D  S  B  M  A  E  L  N  S  A  V
E  L  B  G  Y  Z  I  N  I  L  H  P  K  B
L  A  Y  K  S  W  N  K  S  P  R  I  U  H
G  O  F  V  L  X  T  V  S  N  H  C  K  I
E  B  D  O  E  P  A  W  A  K  U  A  D  W
U  E  Y  V  V  G  K  S  S  I  R  I  U  S
S  A  L  D  E  B  A  R  A  N  J  E  F  Z
E  W  P  O  L  A  R  I  S  L  V  A  X  D
```

DAY 7

don't forget to go back and bubble
in your habit tracker on page 7!

God stopped to party!

Hey, just so you know, you have officially made it to Day 7. What's so important about this day?

Day 7 is a party day.

It has been that way since the beginning of time.
After six days of creating the world, God stopped on the seventh day to celebrate and enjoy everything that had been created.

Did you know that ...
God enjoys watching
you enjoy something
that was created
for you to enjoy?

God created a world so you can ...
swim in the ocean.
run a race.
climb a mountain.
laugh with your friends.
smell the flowers.
taste ice cream.
ride your bike.

YAY!

sing a song.
play a game.
hear an owl.
feel the wind.
watch fireworks.
hold someone's hand.
hug a friend.
jump on a trampoline.
kick a ball.
dance to music.
party under the stars.

God made this world to keep spinning around
and orbit the sun. God actually organized the sun, moon,
stars, and planet Earth so humans could have
days and nights and seasons that change . . .

That's the reason we can have calendars.

And you need a calendar to schedule a party, by the way.
Because every once in a while, it's good to party for a good
reason. When you stop to celebrate something good, it helps you
remember God's goodness.

Every party is celebrating something.
A birthday party celebrates the day someone was born.
A New Year's Eve party celebrates a brand-new year.
A pizza party celebrates eating pizza.

DAY 7   C-E-L-E-B-R-A-T-E good times

There is a reason why God stopped to party when the world was being created. And there's a reason why, for generations, God's people planned special days for feasts and celebrations.

It just so happens that someone was counting stars one night because they didn't realize there were 200 billion trillion stars. This person was so moved by God's goodness and what God had done in the universe that he wrote a song about it. This song was something God's people would often sing when they threw a party:

> Give thanks to the LORD, for he is good.
> *His love endures forever . . .*
> who by his understanding made the heavens,
> *His love endures forever . . .*
> who made the great lights—
> *His love endures forever.*
> the sun to govern the day,
> *His love endures forever.*
> the moon and stars to govern the night;
> *His love endures forever*
> (Psalm 136:1-9, NIV).

So, let's party and celebrate all the good that God has done!

when you stop

to celebrate

something good,

it helps you

remember God's

goodness.

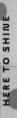

DAY 7

birthday time capsule

To celebrate, let's make a real time capsule that you can open on your birthday!

Scan the QR code and click "Start Here":

1

Choose your container. (This could be a Mason jar, a shoebox, or any other container that you can close up.)

2

Decorate your time capsule with stickers, paint, markers, tape, or glitter.

40

YAY!

3

Add photos from the last year, or cut out pictures from magazines or newspapers that remind you of something from this year, like your favorite food, favorite styles, etc.

4

Include a note to YOU from YOU!

Scan the QR code

5

Include note(s) for YOU from your friends or family. Include as many notes as you want. (But don't look at what they write!)

Scan the QR code

6

Make sure all of these things go inside your time capsule!

P.S. Don't seal your capsule yet because you'll still need to add some more items as you complete this book!

41

the way
the truth
the life

WHEN

JE

What's Ahead This Week

→

DAY 1

Jesus was born for a reason

MADE

DAY 2

WOW!

Wow, look at God

DAY 3

WHAT IF?

Imagine what Jesus did

US

WAS
BORN

DAY 4 LOOK

Follow
the Son

DAY 5

God is
here with
us

HERE

DAY 6

You are
loved

LOVE

DAY 7 YAY!

Jesus
liked
parties

JESUS was born to save the world
He was human and divine
He boldly claimed, "I am the light"
God's Son began to shine

He glimmered and beamed
and burned so bright
God's kingdom from above
and heaven's mirror showed the world
the STORY of God's love

The true bright Morning Star
God sent to show the way
Here to shine, here to say
God is good, God is great

Ancient words illuminate
a promise Jesus made
He lived and died and lived again
So we can celebrate

Hope was born from eternal life
and that love still lights our way
Here to shine, here to say,
God is good, God is great

A long time ago, in a real place called Bethlehem, Jesus was born...

Merry Christmas!

Jesus was God's Son, Who came into this world to . . .

Love. Heal. Forgive.
Guide. Rescue. Save.

Jesus also came to show us how to live . . .
like really, REALLY live.

How would this baby change the world?

Who would He grow up to be?

Someone more powerful and wonderful
than anyone could have ever imagined.

So what did He do? Let's find out together.

45

HERE T
WEEK TWO
HERE TO SHINE
WEEK TWO
HERE TO SHINE
WEEK TWO
SHINE

Jesus was born for a reason

Do you watch the stars?
No. Not the stars in the night sky.
The stars on YouTube.

Just like you can see the Big Dipper from anywhere in the world,
you can see anything a YouTube star does from anywhere in the
world—over and over again.

The world 2,000 years ago was a very different place
from the world you live in today.

Imagine what it would be like if there were no...
YouTube
refrigerators
hoverboards
planes
telescopes
Minecraft®
McDonald's®
electricity

In your world, news travels fast.
In that world, news traveled slow.

WHEN JESUS WAS BORN

Think about it: If we had no phones, how would you let people know when something important happened? Of course, that wouldn't be a problem for God.

If God wanted to tell everyone something, God could . . .
write it on a rainbow.
whisper it in the wind.
send enough angels to tell everyone at once.
instantly create a better internet connection.

But here's something that sounds truly incredible.
When God decided to send a message to the world 2,000 years ago, He didn't create millions of billions of stars again.

God did something even more amazing.
God was born into the world as a baby.
God became a human.
For the first time ever, God had a face.

His name was Jesus.

And when Jesus was born, God sent an angel, but not to tell everyone. The angel told Mary—who would become the mother of Jesus. The angel told her:

> "You must call him Jesus.
> He will be great and will be called the
> Son of the Most High God . . . and will rule forever
> over his people" (See Luke 1:31-33).

47

DAY 1

do you know what we celebrate...

Then God sent more angels,
but not to announce the news to the world—
just to tell a handful of shepherds:

>   "Do not be afraid.
>   I give you good news for all people.
>   A Savior has been born" (See Luke 2:10-11).

And God even made sure there was a
bright morning star in the sky—
not so the world would notice,
but so a few wise astronomers would see it.

Even though these wise men made the mistake
of sharing the news with an evil king,
what they said was revealing:

>   "Where is the one who has been born the king of the Jews?
>   We saw the star when it rose and have come to worship him."
>   (See Matthew 2:2).

So when Jesus was born,
most of the world had no idea that
God had just become human.
But soon the whole world would know
the reason that Jesus was born.

find the north star

1. Connect the dots to reveal the Little Dipper and the Big Dipper.

2. Find the North Star by looking at the Big Dipper. The two stars on the end of the Dipper's "cup" point the way to Polaris, which is the top of the handle of the Little Dipper. Circle it!

5

3

2

6

4,8

1

7

Little Dipper
URSA MINOR

1

2

Big Dipper
URSA MAJOR

3,7

6

4

5

Hint: The North Star is labeled "1" on the Little Dipper.

wow! days can really blow you away!

wow, look at God

Since Jesus was God, that means ...

God lived in a poor neighborhood.
God felt emotions.
God got tired and took naps.
God said, "Ouch."
God had dark skin.
God worked long days.
God fished
and jumped
and walked
and sang
and danced
and laughed.

**God became one of us so that we would know
how close God wanted to be to all of us.**

That's why Jesus said,
"I am the light of the world" (John 8:12, NIrV).

He wanted to shine a light so
everyone would see what God is like.

 WHEN JESUS WAS BORN MADE

And so everyone could see how God sees them.

It's why Jesus said:
"I am the bright Morning Star" (Revelation 22:16, NIrV).

At first, only a few people actually knew Who Jesus was.

But when Jesus showed up as a boy in the temple to have a conversation with adults about what God is like, religious leaders were impressed.

And when Jesus started healing people who were sick, and made a storm stop raging in the sea, the crowds were amazed.

When Jesus would teach how to understand and experience the kingdom of God, everyone who listened was astonished at His words.

The people closest to Jesus started believing that He really was the Son of God.

Here are some of the things they said:

His first cousin John the Baptist said,
"I have seen that this is God's chosen one" (See John 1:34).

DAY 2

when you discover more about Jesus...

James, Jesus' half-brother, identified himself as
"James, a servant of the Lord Jesus Christ" (See James 1:1).
(What do you think it would take to say that about your own
brother or sister?)

Peter, one of Jesus' followers, said,
"You are . . . the Son of the living God" (Matthew 16:16, NIV).

Martha, one of Jesus' close friends, said,
"I know you are the Messiah" (See John 11:27).

People in the crowds who watched Jesus said,
"Never have we seen anything like this in all of Israel"
(See Matthew 9:33).

It's like they were all saying,
"Wow, look at God!"

The closer people got to Jesus, the more
they trusted that He was the Son of God.

But that's why Jesus came.
He wanted to prove to everyone who saw Him,
"If you trust me, you can trust God."

WOW!

WOW

What is it about Jesus that amazes you the most? Say a prayer and thank God for sending Jesus.

WOW! WOW! WOW!

WOW

when you discover more about Jesus...

imagine what Jesus did

There was a story people heard about Jesus for centuries before He was born.

A child will be born to us...
And he will be called Wonderful Counselor, Mighty God,
Everlasting Father, Prince of Peace (See Isaiah 9:6).

People knew that God would send someone to rescue them one day, but they didn't have all the details. What did the promise actually mean?

Wonderful? What if He'll be an influencer?
Mighty God? What if He'll be a legendary warrior?
Prince of Peace? What if He'll be a king?
Everlasting? One of the old, all-powerful magi (you know, one of the magicians, astrologers, and wise men of His time)?

Little did they know that Jesus would show up and do things they could never have imagined.

He ...
defied gravity by walking on water.
disappeared through crowds.
appeared through walls.
made blind men see.
healed the sick.
raised the dead.
fed the hungry ...

Jesus would do things that would break the laws of nature—but then again, He did create nature. Some people started to follow Him because of His miracles.
But He knew they were missing the point.

Jesus wasn't doing miracles to simply impress them with God's power. Every miracle was a statement to His followers about God's love for them. Eventually, the crowds and leaders became so threatened by Jesus' growing popularity that they wanted to get rid of Him.

When that time came, and in front of maybe Jesus' biggest crowd yet, people shouted: "Save yourself! Come down from the cross, if you are the Son of God!" (Matthew 27:40, NIV).

Now Jesus had everyone's attention.
So He did something nobody expected:

Nothing.

DAY 3

use your imagination...

He could have escaped through the crowds. But He didn't.
Or disappeared through walls. But He didn't.
Or defied gravity. But He didn't.
And if He could make a blind man see, surely He could blind a
seeing man so He could escape. But He didn't.

Instead, He died.

And here's what the crowds had missed all along:
Jesus will always do the thing that shows the MOST love.

Jesus could have saved Himself,
but He chose to save the world instead.
And then God proved how much He loved the world
by miraculously bringing Jesus back to life!

When you read the story of Jesus, it's easy to become so amazed
by the miracles that you miss the reason behind the miracles. Jesus
did what He did because He wants you to know that He loves you
like He does. So when you imagine some of the things Jesus actually
did, then maybe you can also imagine what Jesus wants to do in
your life. If God raised Jesus back to life, then Jesus can definitely
help you know how to live life. Maybe that's why Jesus said,

> "I have come that they may have life, and have it to the full"
> (John 10:10, NIV).

WHEN JESUS WAS BORN!

WHAT IF?

imagine Jesus

Think of five or more words that describe Jesus and all that He can do. Write them in the speech bubbles!

57

have you ever had to follow...

follow the Son

Has someone ever said to you: "Trust me?"
You may not realize that most days,
you are choosing to trust someone about something.

Like when you're in the middle of . . .
that 10-step math problem, you trust what the teacher taught you.
that 20-part "how-to" YouTube tutorial, you trust whoever is
explaining what to do.
that 100-page LEGO® instruction manual for the Millennium Falcon
and you're only on bag B-153, you trust the people who wrote the
instructions.

Following Jesus has a lot to do with trust. Jesus' invitation to
everyone could be summed up in two words: "Follow me."
It was His way of saying, "Trust me."

**God, Who designed you and the world around you, became a
human and said, "Follow me." Why not trust the One Who knows
everything about how you were designed?**

Some people followed Jesus for a while,
but they stopped trusting when it wasn't easy . . .
when it got confusing.
when it was taking longer than expected.
when other people's lives looked better than theirs.

But others kept trusting. They stayed close enough to Jesus...
to ask their questions.
to share their frustrations.
to see miracles happen.
to listen to His stories.
to discover joy at dinner parties.

The closer they got to Jesus, the more they saw the reflection of a God Who loved them, regardless. They learned that Jesus could be trusted, because Jesus actually loved them.

It began to make sense to them when Jesus said:

"I am the way and the truth and the life" (John 14:6, NIrV).

Jesus' life was like a compass, pointing the way for you to...

have a relationship with God.
love your neighbors (and your siblings).
experience forgiveness and hope.
shine a light in dark places.
demonstrate the priceless, most valuable things in life, like love, joy, peace, patience, kindness, goodness, and self-control.

Jesus was God's Son. He really did shine a light to show everyone the way to know God. He wanted you to follow Him so you could see something about the world that God wants you to see. Mostly, Jesus wants you to put your trust in Him and know how much He loves you.

DAY 4

you might want to turn your book sideways for this

follow

Fill in the crossword puzzle with the clues below!

ACROSS

1. A ____ is a huge collection of gas, dust, and billions of stars and their solar systems.

3. A group of stars that looks like a shape and has been given a name is called a ____.

4. Jesus called Himself the bright ____ Star. (See Revelation 22:16)

8. ____ is going forward or backward in time.

9. The distance that light travels in one year in a vacuum (or about 5.88 trillion miles) is called a ____-year.

11. The ____ telescope was the first to travel on a rocket ship and take pictures in space.

12. Jesus said, "I am the ____ and the truth and the life." (John 14:6, NIrV)

DOWN

2. ____ are scientists who observe the stars.

5. ____ is the force that creates a star.

6. Jesus performed ____ to prove how much God loved the world.

7. The seven brightest stars in the constellation of Ursa Major that are shaped like a handle are called the Big ____.

10. When Jesus was born, God became ____

ANSWERS

ACROSS 1. Galaxy; 3. Constellation;
4. Morning; 8. Time travel; 9. Light;
11. Hubble; 12. Way

DOWN 2. Astronomers; 5. Gravity;
6. Miracles; 7. Dipper; 10. Human

who do you like to talk to the most?

God is here with us

Have you ever tried to explain something hilarious to someone who wasn't there when it happened?

You retell the story, and here comes the punchline.
You land it *perfectly*. And the other person just kind of chuckles.
You can totally tell. They don't get it.
They just had to be there.

If they had actually been in the room where it happened,
then they would have experienced something entirely different.

Being together can make ...
joy more contagious.
sadness bearable.
anger controllable.
fear face-able.

God actually designed us to be in relationships. It's why God sent Jesus to Earth as a human to walk, talk, and hang out with humans. Jesus came so we could understand that God isn't a distant Creator we can't really know, but that God is Someone Who wants to be in a friendship with us.

When Jesus came, He experienced what we experience:

joy fear disappointment

laughter pain exhaustion

peace

creativity

anger beauty

frustration boredom

imagination

Jesus actually demonstrated what it looks like for God to become a friend because He can relate to us. That means you can actually have a conversation with God as if God is your friend. Think about the different ways you can talk to someone who is really a friend . . .

in stories
in grunts and sighs
in slang
in emojis
in silence
in journals
in pictures

What would it look like if you actually believed you could talk to God like God is actually here?

That's the other thing about "here." Here is close.

DAY 5

do you ever try to talk to God?

The story of Jesus describes how God came close to us.
God came close enough so you can know ...

God understands you.
You can have conversations with God.
You don't have to pretend you are someone else.
You can know that God will always be here for you.

Here when you make the team.
Here when you get cut from the team.
Here for your first best friend.
Here when you break your arm.
Here when you get a C+.
Here when you can't sleep.
Here when you need to say you're sorry.
Here when you want Him to be,
and here even when you forgot.

Jesus is Emmanuel, which actually means "God is with us."
Jesus is here WITH you.
That's one promise you can hold onto forever.

communicate like friends

Below is a feelings wheel that represents your emotions. Use this to share with God how you are feeling as often as you want. There are no right or wrong emotions. You can tell God anything.

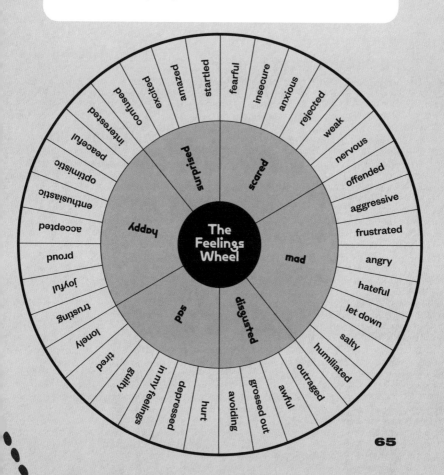

DAY 6

learning about Jesus...

you are loved

Do you use the
word "love" much?

You can love . . .

macaroni and cheese
your grandma
the color purple
Takis®
sneakers
Christmas
unicorns
strawberry ice cream
snow

A lot of times when you use the word "love," you're just
trying to explain how you feel about something or someone.

**Here's something to remember about your feelings:
it can be hard to change how you feel.**

For example, if you don't love unicorns, you can't just make yourself
love unicorns. But if a unicorn were real and you could actually ride
one, then maybe DOING something could change how you feel
about a unicorn.

If it's true that DOING something can change how you feel about something, then doing something FOR someone can change how you feel about someone.

It makes sense, right? If you do something for your friends, it can actually change how you care about them. Maybe that's why Jesus always talked about love as something you do, not just something you feel. Jesus knew that love is an action, not simply an emotion.

Jesus actually said the greatest commandment is to love God with all your heart, soul, mind and strength . . . and to love your neighbor as yourself (See Mark 12:30-31).

Then Jesus told a story to explain what it looks like to DO something for your neighbor.

When Jesus sat down to eat a meal with His best friends right before He died, He gave them a new commandment. He told them . . .

> "You must love one another, just as I have loved you" (John 13:34, NIrV).

What was new about this commandment?
The last part was new: "As I have loved you."

This was the first time God, as a human, explained to other humans how much He loves humans.

DAY 6

discovering how much Jesus loves you...

Jesus told His friends to love each other as He had loved them.

Don't miss this:
Love is not just what you feel.
Love is what you do.

Jesus became human so you could see
how much God loves you.

Jesus became human so you could see
how to love other people.

People who know they are loved
learn how to love other people.

And ...
you are loved.

> The God Who made the stars to shine
> became a human so He could tell you ...
> "I have loved you."

story time

Think of a specific moment in your life when you remember
feeling especially loved by God. What time of year was
it? What other emotions were you feeling? Write that
story down to remember.

Refer back to the feelings wheel on page 65 to help you
name the feelings you were feeling.

_____

_____

_____

_____

_____

_____

_____

_____

_____

Jesus liked parties

It's party day! Remember? It's Day 7 of Week 2.

Remember when God stopped creation for a day to enjoy what He had created? God threw a creation party. Well, God also created you to enjoy what He created.

Maybe that's one of the reasons God created sunlight. Or if we're being scientifically correct, starlight. In case you missed it, the sun is a star. And God not only wants you to enjoy the sunlight; God created the sun to help you enjoy life more.

Did you know that sunlight helps your brain release a chemical that makes you happy, called serotonin? The light from the sun goes through the retina in your eyeball and tells your brain to give you some serotonin! It's a known fact that serotonin increases the happiness of your mood.

So, yeah. The sun can make you a little happier.
But in order to experience the serotonin, you actually have to step outside into the sunlight. You won't enjoy the sun if you don't actually get in the sun.

Did you know that Jesus shone a light to help you find the joy in life? No, Jesus didn't come just to make you happy, but Jesus does want you to discover what makes life meaningful.

Maybe that's why Jesus enjoyed being with people so much. He wanted to see them experience life fully.

Here is something someone who followed Jesus wrote about Him:

> In him was life, and that life was the light of all mankind (John 1:4, NIV).

No wonder Jesus loved parties so much. Jesus liked people. Jesus liked helping people experience life the way God intended. So Jesus showed up at parties, feasts, and celebrations to . . .

show He cared about the things that matter to people.
enjoy life and have fun with people.
give them some good news.
share His light so people could experience life.

By the way, Jesus also gave us some really good reasons to throw some big parties. In fact, there's a good chance that two of your favorite parties every year are all about Jesus.

Jesus holds the title for the ultimate birthday party, Christmas. And every year at Easter, we celebrate what Jesus did for us.

He actually did the unimaginable.
The hardest thing ever.
He gave up His life to show us how much He loves us.

DAY 7

who doesn't love a good party?!

He lived and died and lived again so that we could experience a life that is forgiven and free.

And even when Jesus was on His way to save the world, He stopped and spent time with people to show them how much they mattered to Him.

So if you're looking for a good reason to have a party, just think about what Jesus did.

And remember . . .

**Jesus loved parties
because Jesus liked people.**

Jesus loved parties because Jesus liked people.

DAY 7 plan a party

imagine you are throwing a party for... Jesus!

It could be big or small. You could have lots of food, there could be singing and dancing, or maybe it's just a simple night to watch a movie.

Use the spaces to the right to write things down, draw ideas, and tape in pictures of inspiration!

What do you think would be important to Jesus to do at this party?

What food would you want to have for Jesus?

74

Does the party have a theme?

What is the location
of the party?

List other special things
you will need for the party
(balloons? a cake? DJ or
music?):

Write down the names of who to
invite:

WHEN
Y

What's
Ahead
This
Week

→

DAY 1

You were
born for a
reason

MADE

DAY 2

Wow,
look
at
you

WOW!

DAY 3

Imagine
what you
can do

WHAT
IF?

believe in yourself

U WERE BORN

DAY 4

Discover your light

LOOK

DAY 5

God is here for you

HERE

DAY 6

You are remarkable

LOVE

DAY 7

You were made to party

YAY!

WEEK 3

this section is all about you!

YOU were born to live this life
Wonderfully designed
No wonder God said, "Shine your light"
So this is now your time

To glimmer and beam and burn so bright
Like the stars from above
Be heaven's mirror, show the world
the goodness of God's love

You were born to FIND the way,
and uniquely run your race
Here to shine, here to say
God is good, God is great

Make your mark, illuminate
Live curious and brave
Love to live, live to love
You can pause to celebrate

The wonder and amazement
of a life that God has made
Here to shine, here to say
God is good and God is great

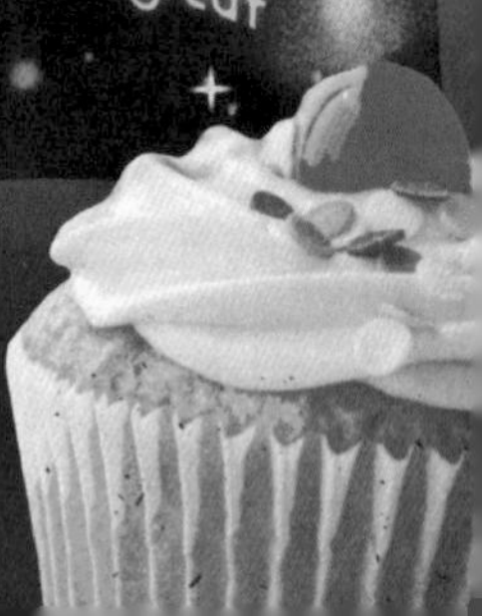

Not so long ago—

___your age___ years ago, to be exact—in a place called ___city where you were born___, YOU were born!

happy birthday!

And instantly, the world changed because you were finally here.

You were born to shine, to celebrate, to become.
Born to rest, to grow, to discover, and to be loved.
Born not just to exist, but to DO and BE SOMETHING every day.

So, what might you do in your wonderful life?
Let's discover together.

79

DAY 1 · just pretend it's your birthday...

you were born for a reason

As we've already discovered, some astronomers believe there are at least 200 billion trillion stars in the sky. And biologists think there are around 7 octillion atoms in the human body.

That's 200,000,000,000,000,000,000,000 stars.
And ... 7,000,000,000,000,000,000,000,000,000 atoms.

Evidently, you were born with a lot of moving pieces. That's why you can build, make, and create so many amazing kinds of things.

You were wonderfully designed, so you can design wonderful things.

That idea was actually written down thousands of years ago. It's in the Bible. David wrote:

> I will praise you, because how you made me is amazing and wonderful (See Psalm 139:14).

Try doing this:
Get up, go look in a mirror, and read this out loud:
"How God made me is amazing and wonderful!"

80

What if you were to start every day by reminding yourself of the way God made you? If you believe that's true about you, then maybe you can convince someone else they are amazing and wonderful too.

Here's something else David wrote to God:

> I think about the heavens.
>> I think about what your fingers have created.
> I think about the moon and stars
>> that you have set in place.
> What are human beings that you think about them?
> (Psalm 8:3-4, NIrV).

Whenever you think about God making the 200 billion trillion stars, remember that God is also thinking about you. That's pretty amazing and wonderful, right?

God, Who created . . .
red birds,
bumblebees,
wildflowers,
evergreen forests,
gray whales,
striped zebras,
snowy mountains,
and blueberries . . .

is actually thinking about you.

DAY 1

God made a lot of amazing things...

Here's something interesting:
God was even thinking about you before you were born.
So there are definitely a lot of reasons God put you here.
God has been thinking about you for a long time.

Read this slowly and see if it makes sense:

**God actually created you to think the way you think
so you could think about God thinking about you.**

Does that make sense?
If you ever wonder if anyone is thinking about you,
you can be sure Someone is: God.

The most powerful,
most creative,
most loving,
most understanding
Someone in the whole world
is thinking about you every night and day.

Think about that!

So go look in the mirror again and say,
"God is thinking about me."

And then go tell someone else,
"God is thinking about you too."

How God made me is AMazing and WONDeRFuL

wonderfully designed

Using a piece of paper and whatever art supplies you love to create with, make a sign to hang on your mirror that says,

"How God made me is amazing and wonderful!"

DAY 2

be sure to look in a mirror today :)

wow, look at you

Wow, look at you!
You are over halfway through this devotional.

Remember how it all started.
At the beginning of the world, God said,
"Let there be light," and the stars began to shine.

Then God became human and said,
"I am the light," and Jesus began to shine.

Then Jesus said something to a crowd on the side of a mountain
one day. What He said will help you see something
about yourself that you may have never seen before:

"Let your light shine."

You were made in such an amazing and wonderful way
that God became human to shine a light
on the light that you need to let shine.

Jesus saw the light that was in people.
He saw the light God had created in everyone.
He saw the light that they didn't even see.

And Jesus said, "Let it shine!"

If you had been standing in the crowd that day, you may have wondered,

"I have a light?"
"Where is it?"
"How do I turn it on?"
"Is there a button or a switch somewhere?"

Jesus was looking at somebody like you and saying,
"Wow. Look at you.
You have a light.
You are here to shine.
Even if you don't know it."

Did you know that God sees your light?
Even if you don't. And even if no one else does.

Have you heard of the James Webb telescope? It's an amazing telescope scientists launched into space in 2021 that has completely changed the way we have been able to see the universe. It takes pictures of stars that we can't see with the human eye.

In 2022, it took an astonishing picture of a star called Earendel— the oldest and most distant star ever seen. Earendel is 50 times the size of our sun, and supposedly over 12 billion light-years away. But the first time we even saw Earendel's light was only in 2018.

DAY 2   keep shining!

The point is, some people believe that Earendel was shining for billions of years before any humans could ever see its light.

But ... God always saw it.

Earendel was there shining, waiting for what seemed like eternity until it was discovered and someone probably said, "Wow look at you!"

Maybe that's what Jesus meant when He said, "Let your light so shine before men, that they may see your good works and glorify your Father in heaven" (See Matthew 5:16).

Jesus never explained how long it may take before someone notices your light. He just wanted you to realize that you have a light that you should shine for a good reason ... so keep shining!

**Just remember, Jesus sees your light.
And He's probably saying right now,
"Wow, look at you shine!"**

let your light shine

Unscramble these words about light
and write them in the blanks.

igllutbhb_____

stra_____

paml_____

glwoctski_____

gtnignihl_____

ujses_____

imagination day...

imagine what you can do

Imaginations are amazing.

They work without even asking for your permission.
Try this: Read the following words and imagine nothing.

Imagine the friendliest dog
with colorful fur
and a nose that changes colors,
eating ice cream,
while balancing on a unicycle.

Imaginations make it possible to see things that don't yet exist.

Imaginations are powerful, and God made you with that special
feature for a good reason! Maybe God invented imagination so it
was always possible to wonder "what if?"

Every good thing always starts with that question, by the way.

WHEN YOU WERE BORN

WHAT IF?

Someone first asked:

- "What if there were another way to heat up food?" And someone invented the air fryer.
- "What if there were a way to use technology without physical buttons?" And someone created the touch screen.
- "What if there were sounds that could make people feel things when you put them together?" Music.

Maybe God gave you an imagination so you could imagine a better future, even when things aren't going your way right now.

Throughout society, people have imagined what they could do and found a way to do it.

- "What if I could build something that would allow me to touch the moon?" Astronaut.
- "What if I could teach people things that can help them change the world?" Teacher.
- "What if I could create videos that help build a community with a shared interest?" YouTuber.

Just imagine what YOU can do!

If you can build the tallest LEGO® tower, then maybe you can engineer the world's tallest building.
If you can take out the trash carefully, then maybe you can invent a way to create cleaner streets for a city.

DAY 3

you were made in God's image...

If you can pray for your sibling when they're afraid or nervous, maybe you can inspire a whole community to discover that God is trustworthy.

Keep asking "what if?" Keep imagining a big world filled with good things. If your infinite imagination is your only limit, imagine what you can do!

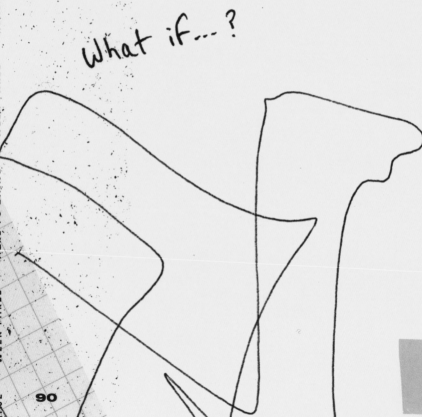

What if...?

WHEN
YOU
WERE BORN
WHAT
IF?

make the world better

1. Find a piece of paper or note card.

2. Invent a job that makes the world
   better by answering these prompts.
   Write your answers on your paper
   or note card.

   Job title
   Age requirement
   What do they do all day?
   How much do they get paid?
   How do they make the world better?
   Draw a picture of them at work.

3. Put this in your time capsule!

TIME
CAPSULE

DAY 4 · God cares about you finding your way

discover your light

Imagination tells us, "Anything is possible! You can do anything!"

But fear says, "Not so fast . . ."

You're too short to play basketball.
Too quiet to be a boss.
Too messy to be a surgeon.
Too afraid of heights to be an astronaut.
Too shy to be on Broadway.
Too weird to start a YouTube channel.
Too weak to be a justice fighter.
Too unorganized to be a vice president.

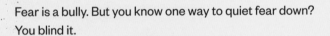

Fear is a bully. But you know one way to quiet fear down?
You blind it.

You shine a light so brightly in its face that it just becomes words,
muttering in the background while you find the bravery to do what
you were designed to do.

You know you were created to do something good, right?
You were created to shine your light. Whether you're a chef,
engineer, athlete, or artist.

No matter what you're working on, as long as your light is shining, you are doing what you were made to do.

Don't let fear dim the light God gave you.
Instead, discover what makes you shine the brightest.
And power it up with everything you've got!

How do you find your light? It's just a little math:

what you're naturally good at +

what inspires you

+ a problem you're passionate about solving

+ your commitment to doing the work

=

Your very good and bright light

Here's the thing. We didn't say it was easy math.

Have you ever watched someone try to start a fire?
It usually goes something like this:

Arrange some logs.
Throw in a lighted match.
Nothing catches.

DAY 4   keep following God's light

Light more matches that fizzle out.
Find some sticks and paper.
Place them carefully in between the logs.
Rearrange the logs. Another match.
This time, a flicker.
Blow on it gently, and it starts to catch.
The wood begins to burn,
and the fire begins to crackle and grow.
Before you know it, you have the warmest, brightest glow,
and you're finally ready to toast (burn) some marshmallows.

Sometimes you just have to work at it.

You may not discover what you are naturally good at until you
try a few things you *aren't* so good at.
You may not find what inspires you until you get inspired.
You may not know what you're passionate about until you get
bored a few times.

But when you find something you're designed to do . . .
Your heart races.
You laugh louder.
Your voice changes.
Your eyes focus in.
You feel that spark, and it shines bright!

And once you discover the light God has given you, any fear you
had that was keeping you from shining it won't stand a chance.

discover
your light

What good things did
your Creator design
you to do?

How can you shine your
light? List some ways
in the stars on this
page!

God is here for you

Who was there on the day you were born?
Do you remember?
Impossible.

Guess what!
God was there.

God was there the moment you let out your first scream,
making your unique voice known to the world.

God was also there for you before that day.
Check this out.

In Psalm 139, David wrote this:

> For you created my inmost being;
>   you knit me together in my mother's womb . . .

> Your eyes saw my unformed body;
>   all the days ordained for me were written in your book
>   before one of them came to be (Psalm 139:13-16, NIV).

Because God made you
and has always known everything about you,
you can be confident that God is *for* you.

That means you can lean on God to encourage you when...

you are annoyed about studying for that science test.
you are super-hangry before lunchtime.
you have to push through another tough practice.
you haven't been the nicest brother or sister.

Because God made you,
and has always known everything about you,
you can believe that God understands you.

Which also means you can lean on God to support you when...

it seems like nothing is going your way.
everything is going your way.
you are nervous about a big choice you have to make.
you are waiting to find out if you made the team.
you make the team.
you don't make the team.
it feels like no one is listening.
you need a friend.

God is here for you.

HERE TO SHI

WEEK THREE

HERE TO SHINE

EK THREE

HERE T

WEEK THREE

SHINE

DAY 5

some things are to be remembered...

write it down

Think of a difficult situation in your life right now.
Write it down so you can remember that God is here
supporting you through it.

Remember

write it down

Write down something in your life that's fun and exciting right now. Don't forget that God is here for you, celebrating and cheering you on!

Don't forget
God is here for you

HERE TO SHI

WEEK THREE

HERE TO SHINE

WEEK THREE

HERE TO SHINE

WEEK THREE

you are remarkable

There are thousands and thousands of little details
about the way you were made
that God remarkably engineered to work together
so you could be you and make a mark.
That's what it means to be remarkable.

From the sound of your voice
to the design of your fingerprints,
to each eyelash on your eyelids,
every little detail was meant for you.

The things that make you nervous and excited,
the things that make you laugh so hard,
and the way emotions send signals to your brain
so that your brain tells your heart to beat faster—
these were all purposefully engineered to make you YOU.

Your heart was the first organ that God made for you.
It beats about 100,000 times in a day and is able to adjust its rate
depending on what your body needs.
It can even sync to the rhythm when you listen to music.

Your body was designed by God to have so many
different experiences.

Think about it:

Your nose can recognize one trillion smells.

Your body contains more than 600 muscles.

Your teeth are just as strong as shark teeth.

When you get hurt, your bones have the power to heal themselves.

God made your brain so impressive that it can:

- store 2,500,000 gigabytes of information (that's like 300 years of TV shows).
- have 50,000 to 70,000 thoughts a day.
- generate between 12 and 25 watts of electricity (speaking of shining, that's enough to power a low-wattage light bulb!).
- think up more than 200,000 questions throughout your life.

God clearly made you with the ability to do and experience some amazing things.

You are here to breathe in the air—

ocean air,

mountain air,

and cookies-baking-in-the-oven air.

And you are here to . . .

tell people you love them,

share hilarious jokes,

sing at the top of your lungs,

and hold your breath to swim.

You are here to ...
learn about the world,
ask lots of questions,
and even change your mind.

And you are here to ...
play games,
make memories,
laugh so hard you can't breathe,
and be a good friend.

You are here to SHINE ...
to make a mark
because you are remarkable.

HERE TO SHINE

WEEK THREE

HERE TO SHINE

WEEK THREE

HERE TO SHINE

WEEK THREE

HERE TO SHINE

make your mark

Draw a picture of something you love, using only dots, marks, or patterns. Some ideas are below! Use this space as a practice area. Then, using your own paper, create your picture and put it in your time capsule!

you were made to party

Have you ever tried to trick yourself? It sounds complicated, right?
Because if you know you're tricking yourself, then you already
know ... so it's not a trick.

Well, here's a trick on how to trick yourself.
The next time you're in a bad mood, smile.
Just try it. Even better, laugh. Do it!

Smiling can trick your brain into being happier.
That's what you call a mind game!
Just another remarkable thing about you to add to the list.
This can come in handy for those days that just aren't going
our way.

God wants us to be joyful. Paul wrote in a letter:

> Always be joyful because you belong to the Lord. I will say it
> again. Be joyful! (Philippians 4:4, NIrV)

God actually made you to party.
This isn't a joke ... (but it's totally okay to smile).
A party doesn't have to be some crazy, over-the-top,
invite-everyone-you-know kind of thing.

WHEN YOU WERE BORN YAY!

It might be a few people you love gathered around the dinner table, or sharing your favorite dessert alone with a parent.
Or maybe the perfect celebration is having your best friend over.

And don't forget, you always have a celebration to look forward to, because you have a birthday every year.
And you know what's crazy?
On your birthday, there are also 17.7 million other people around the world celebrating *their* birthday . . .
giving you millions of reasons to celebrate.

Parties bring people together.
Parties help us celebrate things that matter.
Parties can change how you see life.
Parties are joyful!
When we have fun, laugh, dance, sing, and celebrate together, we are reflecting God's joy to the world. We shine.

God made us to laugh.
Laughter increases infection-fighting antibodies that build up your immune system.
Laughter can decrease pain, stress, and anger.

And when we laugh together, it strengthens our trust and relationships with each other. Just like how Jesus showed up at dinners and celebrations to spend time with people and show them that He enjoyed them, God wants us to do the same.

That's why we were made to party.

105

party on

all about you

Answer these questions about yourself:

What is one of your talents?

What is your favorite season?

What makes you a good friend?

What is your earliest memory?

Would you rather swim or swing?

What makes you laugh?

What is your favorite flavor?

What would your ideal birthday party be like?

Scan the QR code and print out these questions for someone else to answer about YOU! It can be a parent, teacher, coach...

What do you love most about me?

What is one of my greatest talents?

What makes me a good friend?

If you could give me three words you want me to always remember about myself, what would they be?

TIME CAPSULE

WHEN

I

T

Together

DREAM BIG

What's Ahead This Week →	DAY 1 MADE Others were born for a reason	DAY 2 Wow, look at us WOW!	DAY 3 WHAT IF? Imagine what we can do

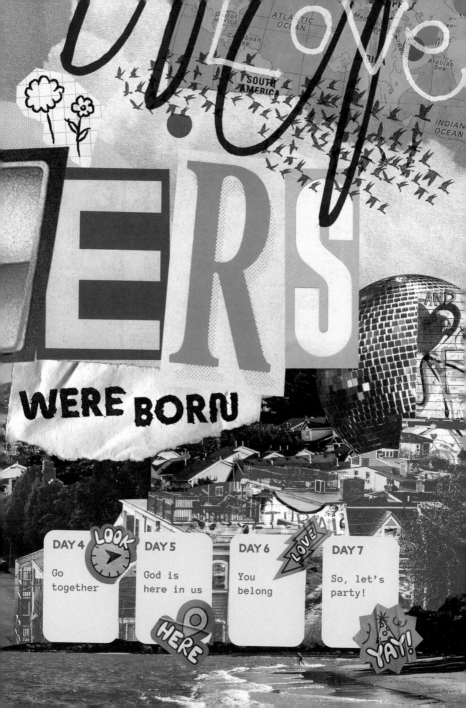

WERE BORN

DAY 4
Go together

DAY 5
God is here in us

DAY 6
You belong

DAY 7
So, let's party!

WEEK 4

only one more week to go.
how's your time capsule?

WE were born to share our lives
Humanity designed
to walk together "in the light"
and give the world a sign

To glimmer and beam and burn so bright
Like galaxies above
We're heaven's mirror to display
the SPIRIT of God's love

Side by side around the world,
called to light the way
Here to shine, here to say
God is good, God is great

Together we illuminate
the Spirit of Christ
We come forgiven and forever free
so we can celebrate

God's symphony of lights
and love we all display
Here to shine, here to say
God is good and God is great

A long time ago, people started being born. And the wild thing is, they never stopped! Seven billion people later . . . we're still going.

Families, and legacies, and tribes, and building societies.
Villages and towns, cities and districts.
Shaping cultures and traditions.
Gatherings and parties of all kinds . . .
All helping us see that "together" is better than apart.
Because together, we can do something good for a good reason.

Through songs and stories, celebrations and rest, generation after generation, the Spirit helps us keep coming back together. We are reminded to care for and celebrate the good in each other. We are reminded to stop and say, "God is good! God is great!"

No matter what, we belong together . . .
because together, we can do something good for a good reason.

DAY 1   imagine all of our lights...

others were born for a reason

Think about something you can't really do by yourself.
It usually takes more than one person to ...

play a soccer game.
sing in a choir.
host a neighborhood party.
rescue people from a flood.
feed families who don't have a home.

It seems like God created us to become a part of something
bigger than any one of us. There really are things we can do better
together. That's why when the world started, God said it was not
good for humans to be alone.

If you look around everywhere you go, you can tell there are
a lot of us. We were all created so we can shine together, not just
by ourselves.

Can you imagine what it would look like if there were only one
star in the sky? The night sky would seem so empty.
There is something magical when all the stars are shining
together, right?

Start counting them. 1 2 3

No, don't. Remember, there are way too many to count.

But what you can do is notice the glow all the stars are making together. They glow because the moon is reflecting the light of our sun—which, of course, is also a star. So, together, the stars and the moon change the way the world looks when they are all shining at the same time.

Jesus actually said that when it comes to our lights, we are like a city on a hilltop that cannot be hidden (see Matthew 5:14). That makes sense, right? We are supposed to be a city of lights to make sure no one misses the glow.

What makes a bigger impression?
One doorway covered in Christmas lights?
Or an entire neighborhood with every house covered in lights?

If more people start shining their lights,
then more people will notice the lights.

When more people notice the lights,
even more people will start shining their lights.

When more of us start showing the world God's goodness,
more people can experience God's goodness.

**When we shine our lights together,
we always make the world a little brighter.**

DAY 1   it's not an accident...

we were born for a reason

Color in some of the windows you see in the city below to make it glow!

DAY 2 all our differences...

wow, look at us

What do you think these things have in common?

Watching a movie
Sending a rocket to the moon
Eating at a restaurant

Here's a hint.
It's not just one thing.

What they have in common
is they all require . . .

Variety.

Producing movies requires a variety of talents.
Sending a rocket to the moon takes a variety of experts.
Restaurants have a variety of food options because people
have a variety of tastes.

**Why do you think people need variety?
Maybe it's because the God who created them
loves variety too.**

Just look at how God created the world.
There are no two stars or snowflakes alike.

116

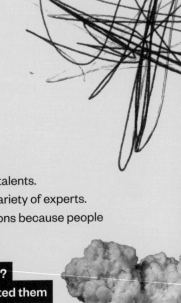

Just look at how God created people.
There are no two people alike either.

It was genius, actually.

God designed humans to be different so they would need each
other. God uses a variety of people to show everyone how much
God loves a variety of people.

That's why God started the Church.

It happened a couple thousand years ago, after crowds of people
had gathered for an annual celebration in Jerusalem called
Pentecost. Everyone who traveled there came from a variety of
countries where they all spoke different languages (see Acts 2).

At Pentecost, God's Spirit showed up like Jesus had promised,
and some amazing things happened.

One thing that surprised the crowd was that when anyone spoke,
everyone else was able to hear what was being said in their own
language at the same time!

Jesus' friend Peter spoke up and explained the story of Jesus.
That day, 3,000 people started believing that Jesus was God's Son
and the light of the world.

When they all went back home to their countries, God's Spirit was with them. That's how churches started showing up in a variety of places. And now churches are everywhere because God's Spirit is wherever there are people who follow Jesus.

It's why John, who also followed Jesus, said,

> When we walk in the light, just as he is in the light,
> then we share life with one another (See 1 John 1:7).

God decided that the best way to shine Jesus' light into the world was to use a variety of people. When we walk together in God's light, we can say, "Wow, look at how God made us! We may be very different, but we are following the same Jesus."

So today, millions of people all around the world are shining God's light as the Church in a variety of places . . . like coffee shops, school cafeterias, gymnasiums, theaters, and even buildings with steeples and stained-glass windows.

Why?

Because people love variety, and God loves a variety of people.

WHEN OTHERS WERE BORN

WOW!

catch the sun

Let's make a "stained-glass" sun catcher!

You will need:
– a paper towel
– a paper plate to trace a circle
– scissors
– washable markers
– a cup of water and a paintbrush

1. Use the paper plate to trace a circle on the paper towel. Then cut out the circle.

2. Color the circle with the markers. You can make the Earth, or design your own planet. Fill in as much of the white paper towel as you can.

3. Dip your paintbrush in water and gently brush over the colors on your paper towel planet.

4. Let your paper towel planet dry.

5. Tape your planet to a window and watch the sun shine through.

Hint: The more colors you use, the more your sun catcher will look like stained glass!

working with each other...

imagine what we can do

No two words will test what you're made of more
than these two words.
Any guesses?

Not "pop quiz" or "low battery." (Never had a pop quiz? Just wait!)

Hint: It's when your teacher puts people TOGETHER and they have
to work on an important assignment TOGETHER and then they
give a big presentation TOGETHER. For a shared grade!

Two words:
Group. Project. (Dun dun dunnnnn.)

Now, it's one thing to work on an easy assignment with people
who are just like you.

▶ Dominate battle mode on Mario Kart with your best friends?
No problem.
▶ Create 20 friendship bracelets before the big concert with
your homies? Easy peasy.
▶ Roll up to recess to play dodgeball with the same friends
you've played with for years? It's going down!!!

But it's a whole other thing to work on something not-so-easy with ALL KINDS OF PEOPLE you never would have chosen to work with.

▶ People who don't look like you and eat foods you've never heard of
▶ People who are know-it-alls
▶ People who think differently than you
▶ People who are kind of mean to other people in the group
▶ People who do the MOST and work too hard
▶ People who are slackers and don't do enough!

Yeah, maybe you can work with them for a few minutes to do something small. But when it's something big like what Jesus wants us to do—like shine our light together—it's more of a challenge. It takes a big imagination and a lot of trust to picture everyone doing their part.

Jesus gave all of us an assignment to do together. As the Church, His people, He wants us to shine our light together by ...

loving God with everything we've got, loving our neighbor, and loving ourselves.

All the time, and as much as possible.

DAY 3

imagine what we can do...

That's a MASSIVE group project. Lucky for us, the assignment has infinite do-overs.

But the BEST part? Jesus never said we had to be the same to work on the same mission.

If one light makes a big difference in the darkness, imagine all of our lights, unique and unified, shining together! Imagine a world with . . .

- ❯ hundreds of focused lasers
- ❯ thousands of guiding flashlights
- ❯ millions of blazing fires
- ❯ billions of captivating spotlights

All shining God's love in the world. What a presentation!

(And don't worry about the grade on THIS group project. You can tell how well we're doing by how much we love each other.)

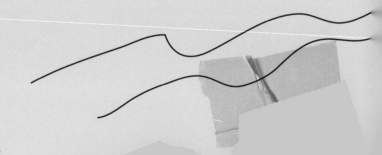

imagine what we can do

Write the name of someone who...
(You can't use the same person twice!)

...has a birthday in July:

_____

...loves math:

_____

...can play an instrument:

_____

...speaks a different language:

_____

...has brown eyes:

_____

...is great at drawing:

_____

HERE TO SHINE

WEEK FOUR

HERE TO SHINE

WEEK FOUR

HERE TO SHINE

WEEK FOUR

TO SHINE

go together

Only three more days to go!

We've been learning a lot from the stars. Now it's time to learn from the starlings.

Find your adult and ask if you can Google "murmuration of starlings." Watch a video about it on YouTube. It's worth your time!

No, a murmuration of starlings is not a massive shape-shifting black cloud. It's hundreds or thousands of small birds, flying together!

For years, it's been blowing people's minds how that many birds stick together and move so suddenly in sync.

Scientists have recently learned how it works. When one bird makes a move, it affects the seven other birds surrounding it, and those birds affect the seven other birds around *them*. And so on and so on, until the entire flock gets the message. Kind of like doing "the wave" in a crowded stadium.

One thing we can learn from looking at the starlings is that if you want to go far, go together.

WHEN OTHERS WERE BORN LOOK

On their long migration journey, starlings rely on each other.

Not just to ...
defend against predators,
provide warmth for each other during a long winter's night,
or share about their favorite bird restaurants ...
but also to make sure they're going the right way!

Can you imagine trying to make such a long trip alone?
How would you know if you took a wrong turn?
Or when you've arrived?
Or which exit to take for the best worm sandwiches (or whatever
you'd eat if you were a starling)?

Together is better. Why? Because ...

We can imagine more together.
Which means we can accomplish more together.
Which means we have more reasons to celebrate together.

Together, our lights ...

- illuminate the way to go when we feel lost and
  remind us that we don't have to go alone.
- point us back toward God, our Creator, when we forget
  all the remarkable things we're capable of.
- help us discover more of what God is like—because,
  remember, each of us has traits of the God who
  created us.

125

DAY 4 guess what!

It's like the starlings read what it says in Ecclesiastes.
(Can birds read?)

> Though one may be overpowered,
>   two can defend themselves.
> A cord of three strands is not quickly broken
> (Ecclesiastes 4:12, NIV).

Whether it's a murmuration of starlings or a gathering of
Jesus-followers, together is better.

What if today you made a decision to be with people as often as
possible . . . so you can lean on, help, and encourage each other?

WHEN
OTHERS
WERE BORN
LOOK

what you bring to the team

Circle the traits below that you're the best at!

Passion

Creativity

Generosity

Patience

Leadership

Fun

Encouragement

Curiosity

Detail

Listening

Kindness

DAY 5   are you glowing?

God is here in us

Did you know that you glow in the dark?
Humans actually emit light.
Go ahead and try it.

Okay, so the light is actually 1,000 times too low for you to see . . .
but like the stars, you do shine. And not just because you emit a
teeny, tiny amount of light.

You actually show the world what God looks like.
Because you were created in the image of God.

**God made humans.
God made you.
You can help the world see what God looks like.**

That's why you can exhibit some of the same qualities as God—
like love, joy, peace, patience, kindness, goodness, faithfulness,
gentleness, and self-control.

And guess what!

You can exhibit these qualities not just because you were created
to be like God, but also because God lives inside you. His Spirit
transforms you and helps you, from within.

That's why you can . . .

be brave even when you are afraid.
be kind even when you are angry.
be patient even when you don't want to wait.
be a peacemaker, even when your brother or sister gets
on your nerves.

When you do these things, you show the world
what God is like.
And like a star, you shine.

And here's the good news: just like you are created in the image
of God, so are other people. Just like God is helping you, God is
helping other people.

So when the world feels dark, and you are looking for the light,
you can look to other people.

- When you need help being brave, you can look to others
  and remember that you aren't alone.
- When you feel sad, you can look to others and find comfort.
- When you feel hopeless, you can look to the people helping
  to remember there is still good.

Because God is transforming and comforting other people,
other people can also comfort you.

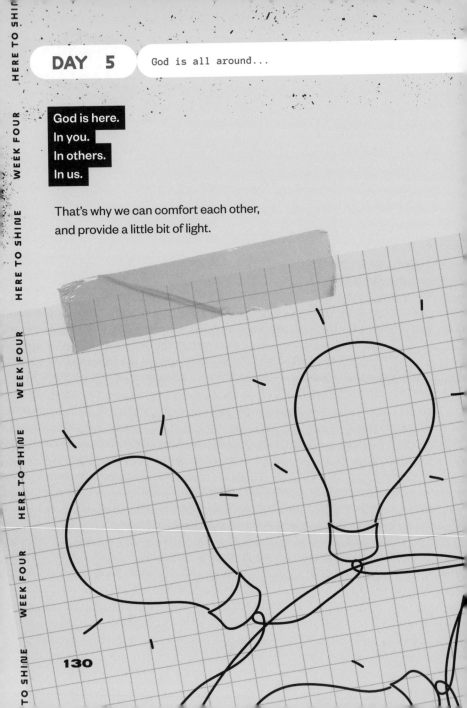

DAY 5

God is all around...

**God is here.
In you.
In others.
In us.**

That's why we can comfort each other,
and provide a little bit of light.

WHEN OTHERS WERE BORN HERE

God is here in us

In the light bulbs, write the names of people who you can trust to comfort you when things are hard.

there is always a place for you

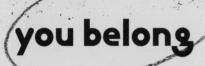

you belong

Close your eyes and picture this for a moment:

It's your first day at a brand-new school. As you arrive in your classroom, your teacher shows you to your desk. You exchange a quick smile with the kid who sits across from you. But you haven't really had a chance to meet anyone. As the morning goes on, a nervous feeling grows in the pit of your stomach. You're dreading it, and it's getting closer:

Lunchtime.

Because who in the world are you going to sit with?
You're too nervous to be bold enough to invite yourself over to anyone's table. And sitting alone seems like absolute torture!

It's noon.

Your class heads to the cafeteria.
You anxiously make your way through the line with your tray.
Just as you exit the kitchen and enter the scary territory of the lunchroom, you hear a few simple words that change the game completely . . .

"Want to sit with us?"

You let out a huge sigh of relief and make your way over to a seat saved for you.

Have you experienced something like that before?

How can something as simple as an invitation to eat at someone's table mean so much?

Because God created us to belong.

Even from the beginning, when the very first person walked the Earth, God recognized that it wasn't good for him to be alone. So God created another human to be there with him.

And God didn't stop there. More and more people were made to live on the Earth together, created with a need for each other and a place in God's family.

We are God's children.
And God's table is huge.
So we can be confident that we all have a seat there.

That means the next time you find yourself in a moment of panic because you don't know where to sit, you can believe that if you're in that cafeteria, there's someone else there who needs you too.

Even if you don't feel like you belong at one table,
there is another table where you do.

DAY 6   `almost party time!`

And in those moments, God is with you,
and you belong to Him.

God is with you when you are ...

looking for a place to sit in the cafeteria.
trying out for a sports team.
auditioning for the play.
looking for a seat on the school bus.
or having an argument with your friends.

**The thing is, we all shine a little brighter
when we know we belong.**

So remember Who created you.
You were meant to be a part of something.
You belong.
And you can help others feel like they belong too.

There's room for all of us at the table.

you belong

Write about a time when someone went out of their way to make sure you felt included.

_____

_____

_____

_____

_____

_____

_____

_____

_____

_____

_____

so, let's party!

It's the last day of this devotional!
You spent 28 days learning all about why you were born
and how you can shine.
Now let's have some fun!

Have you ever been in a situation where you were supposed to be
quiet, but your best friend or sibling giggled and it made you laugh
out loud? Ooops.

That's because laughter is contagious.
You are much more likely to laugh if you hear someone else laugh.
And you are 30 times more likely to laugh if there are people to
hear you laugh than if you are by yourself.

You know what that means?
The best parties need us.
We were all made to party.
Even Jesus liked parties.
As followers of Jesus, our lives can be full of fun and joy!

When you know God, you know how much there is to celebrate.

You have the best news.
You know there is hope for the world.
You get to reflect the light of Jesus.

That kind of light makes others want to be in your light.
And when those lights come together, it's like a bunch of stars
lighting up the night sky, saying,

"This is a celebration!"

Or it's like a bunch of disco balls, with hundreds of little
mirrors reflecting and shining lights in a million different directions,
as if screaming,

"Let's party!!!"

It's already happening all around you!
Every Sunday.
Every Christmas.
Every Easter.
There are so many chances to shine together.

Just like the city on a hill that's so bright it can't be hidden, when
people who follow Jesus celebrate together, they are a party that is
irresistible! A party full of...

Hope
Kindness
Love
Forgiveness
Gratitude
Compassion

137

DAY 7

hey, you did it!

And don't forget . . . FUN!

On Sundays, when everyone is singing the same song or playing a fun game . . .

During Christmas celebrations, when friends and family are together giving gifts and telling stories . . .

When Easter morning comes and you gather around to share a meal together . . .

Look at the people around you and see how they shine. Think about those tiny mirrors on a disco ball reflecting hundreds of lights all over the place, and think to yourself (or say out loud):

LET'S PARTY!

WHEN OTHERS WERE BORN

YAY!

when you know God,
you know how much
there is to celebrate.

DAY 7

that was some serious fun

let's party

1

Guest list!

Make table decoration place cards for the people you want to be at your next birthday celebration!

finish your time capsule

Your life is a celebration! Here are some things to do over the next couple of days to complete your time capsule... so that in a year or so, you can look back and celebrate what you've discovered.

Plan to open your time capsule on your next birthday (or, if your birthday is coming up soon, then the birthday after that).

2

Write yourself a letter.

Make sure you say, "happy birthday," because you'll be opening the time capsule on your birthday. What do you want to make sure you remember in a year? If you had one million dollars, how would you spend it today? What do you think will be different about the future you? Tell yourself anything you want! Seal your letter in an envelope and make sure to put it in your time capsule.

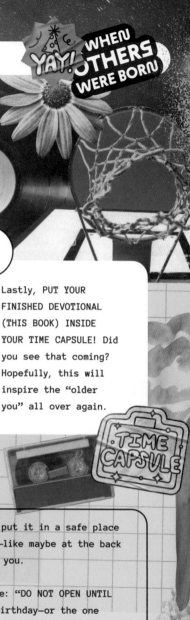

3

Find magazines, stickers, newspapers, or pictures of yourself!

On a piece of paper, create a collage of things that remind you that YOU ARE HERE TO SHINE! Fold or roll up the paper and put it in your time capsule.

4

Lastly, PUT YOUR FINISHED DEVOTIONAL (THIS BOOK) INSIDE YOUR TIME CAPSULE! Did you see that coming? Hopefully, this will inspire the "older you" all over again.

Once your time capsule is complete, put it in a safe place where you'll be able to find it later—like maybe at the back of your closet. Ask an adult to help you.

Write on the top of your time capsule: "DO NOT OPEN UNTIL (month/day/year)" (fill in your next birthday—or the one after that).

NASA
7-148-2272

BYE!

Wow! You made it to the end!

What was your favorite part?!

We hope you know that you were born for a good reason and all of us together are part of God's story. So shine! That's how we follow Jesus' example and start the party everywhere we go.

Now, here's the part where we say goodbye for a little while. Go explore and grow, and discover how powerful it is to . . .

`shine your light!`

See you at your next birthday!

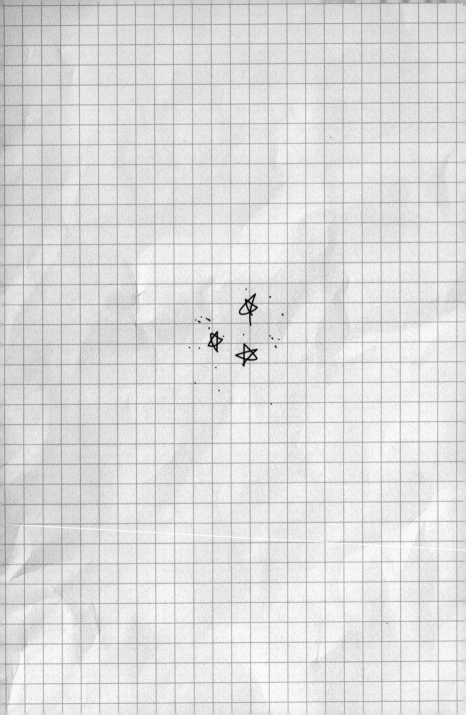